PA

Inside
Government

★ ═══ POLITICAL ═══ ★
PARTIES

Edmund Lindop

TF
CB

Twenty-First Century Books

A Division of Henry Holt and Company

New York

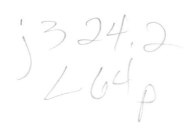

Twenty-First Century Books
A Division of Henry Holt and Company, Inc.
115 West 18th Street
New York, NY 10011

Henry Holt® and colophon are trademarks of
Henry Holt and Company, Inc.
Publishers since 1866

Text copyright © 1996 by Edmund Lindop
All rights reserved.
Published in Canada by Fitzhenry & Whiteside Ltd.
195 Allstate Parkway, Markham, Ontario L3R 4T8

Library of Congress Cataloging-in-Publication Data
Lindop, Edmund
Political parties / Edmund Lindop.
p.   cm.—(Inside government)
Includes bibliographical references and index.
Summary: Provides a history of political parties in the United States, along with insights about their inner workings and the role they play in the politcal process.
1. Political parties—United States—History—Juvenile literature.
[1. Political parties—History.] I. Title II. Series.
JK2261.L56   1996
324.273-dc20   96-11428
                                                                           CIP
                                                                           AC

ISBN 0-8050-4618-6
First Edition—1996

Printed in Mexico
All first editions are printed on acid-free paper.∞
1 3 5 7 9 10 8 6 4 2

Designed by Kelly Soong

Photo credits

pp. 10, 47: AP/Wide World Photos; p. 14 (both): North Wind Picture Archives; p. 20: Culver Pictures, Inc.; pp. 23, 29: The Granger Collection, New York; p. 30: Corbis-Bettmann; p. 37: Brown Brothers; p. 40: UPI/Corbis-Bettmann; p. 49: Mark Peterson/ Saba Press Photos.

☆

To Godfrey "Jeff" Harris, former student,
public policy analyst, successful author, and cherished friend

CONTENTS

ONE
WHY WE HAVE POLITICAL PARTIES

The United States Constitution says nothing about political parties. President George Washington strongly opposed and feared the growth of political parties. In his farewell address as he stepped down from the presidency, Washington compared the strife between political parties to a "fire not to be quenched [that] demands a uniform vigilance lest, instead of warming, it should consume." The first president was deeply concerned that the struggle between parties could lead to mob rule and quite possibly to a dictator capturing control of the government.

At the time when Washington became the nation's chief executive, other American leaders echoed his attitude toward political parties. "There is nothing which I dread so much," declared Vice President John Adams, "as a division of the republic into two great parties, each arranged under its leader." Thomas Jefferson agreed, writing in 1789, "If I could not go to heaven but with a party, I would not go there at all."

Despite all the warnings against their creation, the emergence of political parties in the United States was inevitable. In a democracy, people are free to discuss their opinions and to disagree with one another. When many Americans have similar views about public issues and many other Americans have opposite views, each side organizes its supporters into groups, or political parties.

The chief purpose of a political party is to seek the control of government through the winning of elections and the holding of government offices. Beginning in the early years of the republic, two major parties usually have dominated the American political scene. Since 1854, these two major parties have been the Republicans and the Democrats. Minor parties also have played a significant role in U.S. political history.

Members of a political party join together because they share certain beliefs. Many Republicans share conservative beliefs. Conservatives emphasize respect for traditional institutions and values and generally believe that the best government is the least government. Many Democrats are liberals. Liberals generally approve extending the power of the government in order to bring about changes that they feel will improve society and promote the well-being of its citizens.

Sometimes conservatives are referred to as the group on the political right and liberals as the group on the political left. These terms, *right* and *left*, stemmed from a practice followed by the assemblies of European governments in the eighteenth century. Conservatives sat to the right of the presiding officer as he faced the assembly, and liberals sat to his left.

Republicans today usually favor balancing the federal budget, lowering taxes, and reducing the programs and agencies established by the national government. They also support limiting the terms of national and state legislators, lessening government restrictions imposed on companies, overhauling the welfare system to support only truly needy people, reducing immigration, and curtailing civil rights programs that discriminate against white males.

Democrats today usually favor strict controls on the sale and ownership of guns and other assault weapons, strengthening measures that protect the environment against the pollution of the air and water, and the continuation of programs designed to protect minorities and women against discrimination in the workplace and in the college admissions process. They also argue in behalf of continuing most Medicare and Social Security benefits for the elderly, government programs to provide more jobs for workers and increased educational opportunities for the children of middle-class families, and a welfare system that may undergo changes but still offers a strong safety net for society's poverty-stricken people.

One of the chief issues that separates most Republicans from most Democrats is national power versus states' rights. Republicans generally support turning over to the states many of the programs that have been administered and financed by the federal government. They believe that state and local officials are nearer to the people and have a better understanding of these people's needs and problems. Democrats, on the other hand, argue that these programs are operated more fairly and efficiently by the national government, which can address more impartially the needs and problems of various states. Democrats are concerned that if most of the government finances—except for national defense—are handed over to the states, who will be able to meet the costs of interstate projects or pay to repair the extensive damage caused by widespread natural disasters such as earthquakes, fires, and hurricanes?

All Republicans are not conservative, and all Democrats are not liberal. There are moderate (middle of the road) and liberal Republicans, as there are moderate and conservative Democrats.

Members of a political party do not agree on all issues. Many Republicans, for example, oppose abortion as a practice for ending unwanted pregnancies; other Republicans believe that a pregnant woman should have the right to decide whether she will have an abortion. While a large number of Democrats want to protect forests, parks, and wetlands from commercial use, other Democrats argue that this conservation policy takes jobs away from loggers, ranchers, and land developers.

Political parties try to bring together conflicting groups within their organizations. They attempt to modify and compromise the contending views of their supporters, and thus help to unify rather than divide their members. Both the Republican and Democratic parties want to appear as "friendly umbrellas under which all Americans . . . are invited to stand for the sake of being counted in the next election," said author Frank Smallwood.

An important function of political parties is to help select candidates for public offices. In most states, the members of each party vote in primary elections to nominate their candidates for various offices and to choose delegates to national party conventions. Other states hold their own caucuses (meetings in neighborhood voting districts) or state conventions to select candidates and national convention delegates.

☆ ══════ ☆

A chairperson collects votes at a February 12, 1996,
caucus in Runnells, Iowa. Pat Buchanan won with 26 votes,
Bob Dole had 17 votes, and Phil Gramm had 9 votes.

The delegates to national party conventions nominate presidential and vice presidential candidates. The delegates also create the platform on which their party's nominees stand. This platform is a written statement that explains the party's beliefs and goals—what it stands for and what it hopes to accomplish.

After the candidates have been nominated, each party's chief aim is to have them elected. To attract as many voters as possible, the party helps obtain and pay for time on television and radio for speeches and advertisements. It stages rallies and places ads in newspapers and on billboards. Party headquarters are set up in many cities and towns, and armies of workers phone voters, stuff envelopes with pamphlets, and distribute signs, buttons, and bumper stickers to supporters.

If its candidates are elected, the party prompts these winners to fulfill their campaign promises and perform well in office. If its candidates are defeated at the polls, the party plays a different role. It serves as a vigilant "watchdog" that opposes what appear to be bad bills dealing with current problems, exposes poor administration of laws, and attempts to uncover any evidence of corruption.

Political parties are involved in the elections of many officeholders besides the president and vice president. These include the elections of members of Congress, governors, and many others in state and local governments. All elections in which candidates represent political parties are called partisan elections.

There also are elections in which candidates do not represent political parties. These are called nonpartisan elections. For example, judges are chosen in nonpartisan elections. In many states, sheriffs, district attorneys, and members of boards of education run in nonpartisan elections. Some cities, such as Los Angeles, have mayors selected in nonpartisan elections, while other cities, such as New York, have mayors chosen in partisan elections.

TWO
THE FIRST POLITICAL PARTIES

Political groups known as factions emerged on this country's soil even before the United States was born. The first major struggle between opposing factions involved the Constitution, which was written in 1787. At least nine of the thirteen states existing in 1787 had to ratify, or approve, the Constitution before it could go into effect. Conventions were assembled in the states to vote on whether or not the Constitution should be ratified.

One political faction, called the Federalists, strongly supported the Constitution. Its leaders, including George Washington, Alexander Hamilton, and Benjamin Franklin, believed that the Constitution would provide a powerful central government, which they felt was greatly needed. At that time the national government, known as the Articles of Confederation government, was a loose-knit organization with few powers. Washington sadly described it as a "rope of sand" and observed that "the Confederation appears to me to be a shadow without substance."

Other leaders, such as Patrick Henry, Richard Henry Lee, and George Mason, opposed the ratification of the Constitution and were called Anti-Federalists. They feared that a strong national government could wipe out the powers of the states and favor wealthy individuals at the expense of common people. Also, the Anti-Federalists attacked the Constitution because it contained no bill of rights to protect people's liberties against any tyrant who might arise under a powerful national government.

The battle over ratification of the Constitution was intense, and the voting in some state conventions was very close. But on June 21, 1788, New Hampshire became the ninth state to ratify the Constitution, and the new government began operating on March 4, 1789. Two years later, in 1791, the Bill of Rights was added to the Constitution as its first ten amendments.

As expected, George Washington was elected president with no opposition. Following his first term, he wanted to retire to his home at Mount Vernon, Virginia. The public, however, insisted that he stay in office, and Washington was again elected unanimously.

During the first president's administration, two opposing political parties developed. The more conservative party, headed by Alexander Hamilton and John Adams, kept the name Federalist. The more liberal party, led by Thomas Jefferson and James Madison, was called the Democratic-Republican Party. (Its members also were known as Republicans, but their party should not be confused with the modern Republican Party that began in 1854.)

The Federalists and Democratic-Republicans had conflicting beliefs. The Federalists felt that a strong national government was essential to unite and stabilize the country, provide law and order, and pay back the infant nation's huge debt that resulted from the Revolutionary War. They wanted the direction of the government put into the hands of prosperous, educated men who would rely on their knowledge and experience to govern wisely and unselfishly. Many Americans in 1789 had not gone to school, and Federalists feared that the uneducated poor people might fall prey to radical rabble-rousers or dictators who promised them rewards in return for their support.

Democratic-Republicans opposed the aristocratic views

☆ ════════ ☆

Alexander Hamilton (left) *was one of the heads of the Federalist Party, and Thomas Jefferson* (right) *was a leader of the Democratic-Republican Party. Both parties developed during George Washington's administration.*

of the Federalists and demanded that the national government's power be limited. The bulk of the power, Jefferson declared, should be retained by the states and the people. He insisted that rule by the people was absolutely necessary in a democracy. Admitting that a large number of Americans were illiterate, Jefferson said that the solution to this problem was to educate these people, and then they could play an active part in their government.

Hamilton and other Federalists believed that the United States would someday become a great industrial nation. Their support came mainly from manufacturers, bankers, merchants, and shippers who transported products to and from foreign countries.

In 1789 about 95 percent of Americans lived on farms or in small towns. Jefferson and other Democratic-Republican leaders felt that much attention must be given to the needs and problems of farmers. Most plantation owners in the South and many who owned small farms joined the Democratic-Republican Party. So did large numbers of artisans and craftsmen, such as carpenters, masons, and shoemakers.

The first contested races for the presidency and vice presidency occurred in 1796. The Federalists selected Vice President Adams as their presidential nominee and Thomas Pinckney of South Carolina as their vice presidential candidate. The Democratic-Republicans chose former Secretary of State Jefferson to run for president and Aaron Burr of New York for vice president.

Members of both parties made vicious charges against their foes. Democratic-Republicans accused Adams of being "a friend of monarchy" who was plotting to make his sons "lords of the country." Federalists called Jefferson an atheist, a coward, and a trickster and said his supporters were "cut-throats who walk in rags and sleep amidst filth and vermin."

The framers of the Constitution did not want the ordinary people to vote directly for president and vice president. Instead, they created an unusual electoral device called the electoral college, which still exists. The electoral college consists of electors, who cast the only official votes in presidential elections. Every state is entitled to one elector for each member it has in Congress. The District of Columbia has three electoral votes.

The states decide how their electors will be chosen. In 1796, there were sixteen states; in ten of them, the presidential electors were chosen by state legislatures. Only six states held elections in which the electors were selected by the popular (people's) votes.

Each elector was entitled to cast two votes. The Constitution makers expected that the best qualified candidate would get the most votes and become president and that the second-best candidate would get the second-most votes and be elected vice president. This system worked well in the first two presidential elections, in which every elector cast one vote for Washington. Adams won the second-most votes and became vice president.

The framers of the Constitution, however, had not anticipated the emergence of political parties. Their system for selecting the two highest officials in the national government showed its flaws in 1796. Adams, the Federalist, was elected president with 71 electoral votes; Jefferson, the Democratic-Republican, finished in second place with 68 electoral votes and became vice president. This was the only time in the history of presidential elections that the president and vice president were chosen from opposing political parties.

In the 1800 election, the electoral system ran into another problem. Adams and Jefferson competed again for the presidency. This time Jefferson led with 73 electoral votes to Adams's 65. But Jefferson could not immediately claim victory because all of the Democratic-Republican electors had cast one of their two votes for him and their other for the party's vice presidential candidate, Aaron Burr. So Jefferson and Burr tied with 73 electoral votes each.

According to a provision in the Constitution, this deadlocked presidential election had to be decided by the House of Representatives, in which each state had one vote. Some of the Federalists, who controlled more than half of the seats in the House, preferred Burr to Jefferson, even though it was widely known that Jefferson was the presidential candidate and Burr the vice presidential candidate.

To win the election, Jefferson had to acquire the votes of a majority (at least one more than half) of the states. In the early balloting in the House of Representatives, eight of the sixteen states voted for Jefferson and six voted for Burr. The representatives of Vermont and Maryland were equally divided, so these states lost their votes. Jefferson needed only one more state, but for thirty-five ballots Burr's supporters refused to budge. Finally, on the thirty-sixth ballot, the deadlock was broken when a few Federalists did not vote. The presidency went to Jefferson. The final tally showed that Jefferson won ten states, Burr won four, and two were divided.

The possibility of future electoral-vote ties between a party's presidential and vice presidential candidates was ended by the Twelfth Amendment to the Constitution, which was adopted in 1804. It provided separate elections for president and vice president.

The 1800 election of Jefferson and a Congress controlled by the Democratic-Republicans marked the first time in the history of the United States that the power to govern had changed hands from one political party to another. Jefferson had described the election results as a "revolution," a term that frightened many Federalists. They knew that in some countries when people revolted against their government, it often led to bloody battles and sometimes to the rule of tyrants.

Jefferson, however, was referring to a peaceful revolution. In his inaugural address, he declared, "We are all Republicans; we are all Federalists." The new president explained that despite their distrust of centralized power, he and his supporters did not intend to destroy the national government, and despite their distrust of democracy, the Federalists now understood that government decisions must reflect the will of the people.

Jefferson's belief that people in a democracy would not resort to violent revolution should their party lose an election became one of the enduring features of the American political system. The only exception to this longstanding tradition occurred in 1861, when the Civil War between the North and the South broke out following Abraham Lincoln's election to the presidency.

THREE
POLITICAL PARTIES
1804–1856

From 1801 to 1825 the White House was occupied by presidents from Virginia: Thomas Jefferson, James Madison, and James Monroe. Each of these three Democratic-Republicans served two terms as president.

The popularity of the Federalist Party declined sharply as growing numbers of Americans became convinced that it catered to the interests of prosperous people. The Federalist presidential candidate in 1804, Charles C. Pinckney, won only 14 electoral votes to Jefferson's 162.

During the War of 1812 against Great Britain, the Federalist Party almost committed both treason and suicide. The war was very unpopular with merchants and shippers in New England who depended on trade with Britain for much of their income. In 1814 some New England Federalists threatened to pull their states out of the Union. This threat ended, however, with the coming of peace in 1815. After the war, many Federalists were scorned as traitors. Their party made a feeble, unsuccessful attempt to win the presidency in 1816 and then died.

Following the War of 1812, an astonishing spirit of national unity spread across the country and had a strong impact on the political system. For a brief period the United States was a one-party nation. With the Federalist Party dead, there was no other political party to oppose Democratic-Republican President Monroe when he ran for a second term in 1820.

Like Washington, Monroe would have won a unanimous vote in the electoral college except for a stubborn New Hampshire elector named William Plumer. He cast his vote for John Quincy Adams, son of John Adams. When asked why he had deprived Monroe of a unanimous reelection victory, he sternly replied, "Mr. Monroe, during his last four years has, in my opinion, conducted [himself] as president very improperly."

Four Democratic-Republicans competed for the presidency in 1824. In previous elections every presidential candidate had been nominated by a congressional caucus, which was a meeting held by members of Congress who belonged to the same political party. The 1824 congressional caucus selected Secretary of the Treasury William H. Crawford of Georgia as its nominee. Crawford, however, was not a popular choice in all regions, so state legislatures nominated three other candidates. Henry Clay was the candidate of Kentucky, and John Quincy Adams was the choice of Massachusetts and other New England states. Tennessee nominated General Andrew Jackson, who had become a popular hero after leading troops in the War of 1812.

The first time that careful records were kept of the nationwide popular vote occurred in the 1824 election. It would seem fair and logical to expect that the candidate who wins the most votes cast by the people should be elected president. But this does not always happen, since only electoral votes determine the winner. In three elections, including the one in 1824, the candidate with the most popular votes did not win the presidency.

Jackson won the popular vote in 1824 by a margin of more than 38,000 votes over Adams, his nearest rival. When the electoral votes were counted, Jackson had 99, Adams 84, Crawford 41, and Clay 37. Since no candidate won more than half of the electoral vote, the House of Representatives had to elect the president.

According to the Twelfth Amendment, the names of only the top three candidates—Jackson, Adams, and Crawford—were placed before the House. Clay was eliminated from consideration, but he held the powerful position of Speaker of the House and urged his colleagues to support Adams.

To win the House election, in which each state had one vote, Adams needed the votes of thirteen of the twenty-four states. He felt certain of twelve votes but was one vote short of victory. The New York delegation of House members appeared evenly divided, which meant that New York would have to forfeit its vote when the roll was called.

One New York congressman, Stephen Van Rensselaer, was undecided whether to cast his ballot for Adams and thus break the deadlock in his state's delegation. "The election turns on my vote," he reportedly said. "This is a responsibility I cannot bear. What shall I do?"

☆ ══════ ☆

Stephen Van Rensselaer represented New York in Congress from 1822 to 1829. He also founded a school that later became Rensselaer Polytechnic Institute.

Van Rensselaer bowed his head in prayer, seeking divine guidance. When he opened his eyes, he saw a discarded Adams ballot at his feet. Believing this a divine sign, he picked it up and dropped it into the ballot box. New York then cast its vote for Adams, and the candidate who was runner-up in both the electoral vote and the popular vote moved into the White House.

Infuriated by the 1824 election results, Jackson's supporters charged that their candidate had been robbed of the presidency. They soon began plotting to gain revenge in the next presidential election. This goal was accomplished in 1828, when Jackson received 178 electoral votes to 83 for Adams.

Although no longer a common man because of the wealth and fame he had acquired, Jackson became the symbol of the common people. Born into a poor family, he had achieved success through his own painstaking efforts. He was the first example of what was to become the cherished, often-repeated presidential success story—"from log cabin to the White House." Also, this Tennessean was the first president from a frontier state, and he usually supported causes favored by most Westerners who owned small farms.

While Jackson was president, he and his followers became known simply as Democrats. Before the 1832 election, the Democratic Party held its first national convention. Jackson already had been nominated for a second term by various state legislatures and conventions. The Democratic National Convention nominated Jackson's vice presidential running mate, Martin Van Buren of New York.

Jackson's opponent for president in 1832 was Henry Clay, the candidate of the short-lived National Republican Party (which died after this election). The popular president from Tennessee, fondly nicknamed "Old Hickory," won in a landslide, amassing 219 electoral votes to Clay's 49.

By the time that Old Hickory stepped down from the

presidency, a new political party had begun. Its members had one thing in common—a fierce hatred of Jackson. They called him "King Andrew" and accused him of acting like a dictator and being partial to small-farm owners and city laborers. They chose the name Whigs for their new party because it had been a term used in the Revolutionary War by the opponents of royal tyranny.

Although the Whigs were a rising political force, the party lacked national unity as the 1836 election approached. So instead of nominating a national candidate for the presidency, the Whigs ran three regional candidates nominated by state legislatures. They hoped that the regional candidates together would receive enough electoral votes to throw the presidential election into the House of Representatives, where the party could then unite behind the candidate with the most votes.

The strategy backfired. The Democrats nominated Vice President Van Buren for the presidency, and he won 170 electoral votes compared to a combined 113 for the three Whig candidates. In 1837 outgoing President Jackson handed the keys to the White House to his vice president. (Since then, the only time that a president was immediately followed into office by his vice president occurred in 1989, when retiring President Ronald Reagan was succeeded by Vice President George Bush.)

In 1840 the Whigs nominated General William Henry Harrison for president. He had first won fame in 1811 for leading a battle against Native Americans at Tippecanoe, a site on the Wabash River in what is now Indiana. Harrison's home was in Ohio, and he was regarded as a candidate from the Midwest.

Eager to win votes in the South, the Whigs selected as their vice presidential nominee John Tyler of Virginia, a former Democrat. The 1840 election produced the nation's first famous political slogan: "Tippecanoe and Tyler Too."

The Whigs captured the voters' attention with huge rallies, torchlight parades, fireworks, and campaign songs. Support-

The cover of an old almanac promoting the Whig candidate,
William Henry Harrison, for president in 1840

ers waved Tippecanoe flags, wore Tippecanoe badges, blew
their noses in Tippecanoe handkerchiefs, and washed with
Tippecanoe soap. Men and boys rolled a large ball from Kentucky to Baltimore, Maryland, as a symbol of the majority of
votes the Whigs believed they were rolling up.

When a Democratic journalist sneered that all Harrison
was fit for was to sit in front of a log cabin and drink hard cider,

Whig politicians turned this insult to their advantage. They falsely portrayed Harrison, who was wealthy, as a poor frontiersman. The public was treated to parades featuring log cabins on wheels, where thirsty voters could drink hard cider as they cheered for Old Tippecanoe.

The Democrats nominated President Van Buren for a second term, and he became the victim of nasty personal attacks. Whigs charged that the president was a champagne-drinking aristocrat who sprayed his whiskers with French cologne, wore a corset, ate French food with golden spoons from golden plates, and rode in a British-built gilt carriage.

While the Whigs were staging their massive campaign for Harrison's election, the party chieftains carefully tried to prevent their candidate from making any statements that might lose him votes. Nicholas Biddle, a prominent Whig, advised that Harrison should not be allowed to "say one single word about his principles or his creed. . . . Let him say nothing, promise nothing. Let no committee, no convention, no town meeting ever extract from him a single word about what he thinks now or what he will do hereafter."

The Democrats also held rallies and marched in parades, but they were outshone by the Whigs' more colorful campaign. Harrison won the election with 234 electoral votes to 60 for Van Buren, but the popular vote was closer: The Whig nominee won about 53 percent, and the Democratic nominee about 47 percent.

The excitement of this campaign caused voter turnout to soar. Twelve years before, when Jackson was elected president, only a little more than 50 percent of the eligible voters went to the polls, but in 1840 nearly 80 percent of eligible voters cast their ballots.

When sixty-eight-year-old Harrison was sworn into office on the steps of the Capitol, he delivered an inaugural address that lasted one hour and forty-five minutes, the longest on record. Refusing to wear an overcoat or hat on this chilly day, the new president caught a cold. He developed pneumonia and died exactly one month after his inauguration.

John Tyler was the first vice president to become chief executive after a president's death. Before long, the Whigs realized they had made a serious mistake in nominating this former Democrat for vice president in order to gain Southern votes. Tyler opposed most of the policies favored by the Whig Party. Within a few months all of his cabinet resigned, except for Secretary of State Daniel Webster.

In 1844 the Democrats regained the presidency with the election of James K. Polk, former governor of Tennessee. Polk served four years and refused to run for a second term.

The Whigs rebounded in 1848 and elected Zachary Taylor of Louisiana to the presidency. Like Harrison, Taylor was a general, having achieved fame for his military leadership in the Mexican War. Also like Harrison, he died in office; Vice President Millard Fillmore then became president.

The 1852 election rang a death knell for the Whig Party. In that year they ran their last presidential candidate, General Winfield Scott, another hero from the Mexican War. The Whigs could not wage a winning campaign, largely because of the deep division between their proslavery and antislavery factions. Democrat Franklin Pierce of New Hampshire won the election, but he proved to be a weak president.

Another Democrat, James Buchanan, was elected president in 1856. His administration was badly tarnished because Buchanan failed to deal effectively with the slavery issue that was threatening to tear apart the Union.

FOUR

POLITICAL PARTIES
1856–1932

An act of Congress triggered the birth of the Republican Party. The Kansas-Nebraska Act of 1854 permitted settlers in the Kansas and Nebraska Territories (which were not yet states) to decide whether or not they would allow slavery. This new law overturned the Missouri Compromise of 1820, which had prohibited slavery north of 36°30' latitude. If the people in the Kansas and Nebraska Territories approved, slave owners could then bring their black workers into land that the Missouri Compromise had promised would be forever "free soil."

The Kansas-Nebraska Act enraged antislavery leaders, and some of them were determined to form a new political party to fight the extension of slavery. Northern Whigs, antislavery Democrats, abolitionists, and members of the small Free Soil Party met at Ripon, Wisconsin, to create the Republican Party in 1854. Abraham Lincoln of Illinois soon joined their growing numbers.

In 1856 John Charles Frémont, who had been an explorer, soldier, and California senator, was chosen by the Republican National Convention as its first presidential nominee. Considering that his party was only two years old and that ten Southern states refused to put his name on their ballots, Frémont ran a surprisingly strong race, carrying eleven of the fifteen states in the North and Midwest. Frémont captured 114 electoral votes to 174 for Democrat James Buchanan, the victorious candidate.

The young Republican Party nominated Lincoln for the presidency in 1860. Lincoln's previous experience in the national government had been limited to one term in the House of Representatives, from 1847 to 1849. He ran against Democrat Stephen A. Douglas for a Senate seat in 1858, and the two candidates engaged in a series of debates in several Illinois towns. Although Lincoln lost the election, he gained widespread attention from the debates.

The Democratic Party in 1860 was hopelessly divided between its Northern antislavery and Southern proslavery factions. The Northern Democrats held a convention that nominated Douglas for the presidency; the Southern Democrats held a separate convention that nominated Vice President John C. Breckinridge of Kentucky for president. A fourth candidate, former Senator John Bell of Tennessee, also entered the race. He represented the small Constitutional Union Party. Its leaders were determined not to let the slavery issue cause the Union to be divided into two separate nations.

Lincoln received a large winning margin in the electoral college. He had 180 electoral votes to Breckinridge's 72, Bell's 39, and Douglas's 12. In the popular vote, however, the results were closer. Lincoln had only 39.82 percent of the popular vote to 29.46 percent for Douglas, 18.09 percent for Breckinridge, and 12.61 percent for Bell. Probably the most beloved of all American presidents, Lincoln had the lowest percentage of the popular vote of any victorious presidential candidate in political history!

Shortly after Lincoln's inauguration, the Civil War began, pitting the North against the South, which had seceded from the Union and was now known as the Confederacy. Month after month, year after year, the war dragged on, with neither side able to deliver a knockout blow.

Some Northerners, frustrated by the lengthy warfare and rising number of casualties, wanted Lincoln to seek a truce that would have permitted the Confederacy to continue as an independent nation. But Lincoln was determined that fighting must not cease until the Union was restored. He knew, however, that this courageous stand would cost him many votes in the 1864 election and doubted that he would be elected to a second term.

Republican Party leaders were so fearful of losing the 1864 election that they adopted a strategy to reach out to the so-called War Democrats, voters who considered themselves Democrats but whose first priority was the North's winning the war to restore the Union and free the slaves. The name Republican was dropped by the party for this one election, and in its place was substituted a new one—the Union Party. Former Senator Andrew Johnson of Tennessee, a War Democrat loyal to the Union, was selected as Lincoln's vice presidential running mate.

The Democratic Party adopted a platform calling for an immediate end to the war and a negotiated peace. Its candidates were General George B. McClellan for president and Congressman George Pendleton of Ohio for vice president.

Shortly before the election, the Northern forces won some major battles, which led many voters to conclude that the war would soon end in a Northern victory. This new spirit of optimism helped Lincoln and Johnson defeat their Democratic opponents at the polls.

Lincoln was inaugurated for his second term in March 1865. The following month, two significant events occurred: the South surrendered, ending the Civil War, and the president was assassinated. Vice President Johnson became the chief executive, but he soon ran into serious trouble with Congress. Johnson wanted to follow a lenient policy in restoring the Southern states to the Union. Congress, led by a powerful group called Radical Republicans, demanded much harsher treatment of their defeated foes. The bitter fighting between a stubborn president and a vengeful Congress led to an attempt to remove

☆ ══════ ☆

In an appeal to Northern Democrats during the
Civil War, the Republican Party changed its name
to the Union Party for the 1864 election.

Johnson from office, which failed by only one vote when the
Senate balloted on impeachment charges. The Radical Republicans won their battle to impose severe conditions on the conquered South. They also elected their candidate, General
Ulysses S. Grant, to the presidency in 1868 and again in 1872.

The Republican Party became the country's dominant
political organization. Beginning with Lincoln's triumph in

1860, Republicans held on to the White House and often controlled Congress for the next seventy-two years, except for sixteen years in which Democrats Grover Cleveland and Woodrow Wilson each won two terms as president.

Thomas Nast, a political cartoonist for *Harper's Weekly*, created the Republican Party's symbol, the elephant, in 1874. He also first drew the Democratic donkey.

The Republican Party acquired its famous nickname—Grand Old Party, or GOP—in the 1880s. This was a rather strange nickname, since the Grand Old Party was actually about fifty years younger than the Democratic Party of Andrew Jackson.

Some of the presidential races won by Republicans were very close contests, and one produced an angry dispute. On

TRYING TO KICK IT OVER.

☆ ══════════ ☆

Cartoonist Thomas Nast originated the elephant as the political symbol of the Republican Party in 1874. The elephant and the Democratic Party's symbol of a donkey have appeared in many cartoons.

election day in 1876, it appeared that Democrat Samuel J. Tilden, governor of New York, had defeated Republican Rutherford B. Hayes, governor of Ohio. Tilden led Hayes by more than 250,000 popular votes and had 184 electoral votes—only one fewer than the 185 needed for victory. An additional nineteen electoral votes, almost entirely from the states of South Carolina, Louisiana, and Florida, were disputed and had not yet appeared in the official tally. Both Democrats and Republicans in these states charged that members of the other party had been guilty of intimidating voters and also reporting false returns based on stealing ballot boxes or stuffing them with the ballots cast by ineligible voters.

Congress set up a special fifteen-member electoral commission to investigate the disputed returns. The commission included seven Democrats, seven Republicans, and one other member who, although a Republican, was a Supreme Court justice considered to be neutral about the dispute. Voting along straight party lines, the commission decided by a margin of eight to seven that Hayes was entitled to all nineteen disputed votes. This gave him a total of 185 electoral votes to Tilden's 184, and he eked out a Republican victory in what most historians believe was a stolen election.

In 1880 Republican Congressman James A. Garfield of Ohio easily trounced Democrat Winfield Hancock in the electoral vote, 214 to 155. But 9,210,420 citizens trooped to the polls, and Garfield's margin of victory in the popular tally was a mere 1,898 votes. Never in the history of presidential elections was a popular vote so close!

The Democrats finally broke the GOP stranglehold on the White House by electing Governor Grover Cleveland of New York to the presidency in 1884. Four years later, however, Cleveland lost his bid for a second term to Republican Benjamin Harrison, former senator from Indiana. Like Jackson in 1824 and Tilden in 1876, Cleveland won more popular votes than his rival, outpolling Harrison by more than 90,000 votes.

Harrison, however, carried the four largest states, which helped him win a majority of the all-important electoral vote.

In 1892 Cleveland staged a rematch with Harrison and this time defeated him. When Cleveland returned to the White House, he became the only president to serve a second term that did not immediately follow his first term. He thus became both the twenty-second and twenty-fourth president.

As the end of the nineteenth century approached, the most colorful campaigner of either major political party was William Jennings Bryan, a former Nebraska congressman. He supported a variety of reform measures, but he achieved widespread attention for demanding the free and unlimited coinage of silver, generally known as "free silver." At that time, gold was the only standard upon which coinage was based. Silver was worth much less than gold, so if debtors could pay off what they owed in silver instead, they could save money.

The thirty-six-year-old Bryan addressed the 1896 Democratic National Convention and ended with the ringing words, "You shall not crucify mankind upon a cross of gold!" This remark brought the cheering delegates to their feet, and they nominated him as their presidential candidate.

Bryan's Republican opponent was William McKinley, governor of Ohio. He charged that Bryan was a dangerous radical and strongly condemned his demand for "free silver."

In most previous presidential campaigns, the nominees of both parties stayed at home and let their supporters speak for them at rallies. The candidates believed it was undignified for persons seeking the highest office to travel long distances in order to plead for votes from boisterous crowds.

McKinley followed this long-accepted tradition. He stayed at his home in Canton, Ohio, and waged a "front porch" campaign in which he met with sympathetic groups that had been brought to Canton by special trains. Ample funds were contributed to his campaign by banks, insurance companies, and industrial corporations.

Bryan, on the other hand, took long campaign trips that zigzagged across much of the nation. He traveled 18,000 miles, mainly by train, made more than 600 speeches, and addressed more than 5 million people. Bryan had limited funds, mainly small contributions from farmers and urban laborers.

Despite his exhaustive campaign, Bryan lost the 1896 election to McKinley. Four years later, these two candidates again ran against each other. In 1900 McKinley defeated Bryan by a larger margin of both electoral and popular votes than he had in 1896.

McKinley was assassinated during his second term, and Vice President Theodore Roosevelt was elevated to the presidency in 1901. At the age of forty-two, Roosevelt was the youngest of all presidents. Dynamic and zealous in pursuit of reforms, he became the most popular chief executive since Lincoln. In 1904 he had no difficulty defeating Democratic presidential nominee Alton B. Parker in a landslide.

The Republicans ran Secretary of War William Howard Taft in the 1908 presidential election. Bryan was the Democratic Party's nominee. When Taft won this election, Bryan became the only Democratic presidential candidate who was a three-time loser.

The GOP's chain of triumphs was broken in 1912, when two Republicans ran for the presidency against one Democrat, Governor Woodrow Wilson of New Jersey. Both Taft and Roosevelt vied for their party's nomination at the Republican National Convention. When Taft won the convention battle to represent the GOP in the election, Roosevelt was nominated by the Progressive Party. Wilson won this election that had three major candidates. (This election is covered in more detail in chapter 6.)

By the time that Wilson ran for reelection in 1916, the Republicans were again united. They nominated former Supreme Court Justice Charles Evans Hughes for president. The contest was extremely close. Wilson was not declared the winner until two days after the election, when the returns from California showed that he had won that state and thereby a second term in the White House.

The Republicans were back in control during the 1920s. Their presidential candidates, Warren G. Harding (1920), Calvin Coolidge (1924), and Herbert Hoover (1928), all won easy victories in the so-called Roaring Twenties.

FIVE
POLITICAL PARTIES SINCE 1932

The country was in the midst of the Great Depression at the time of the 1932 presidential election. With many industries and banks shut down, the economy seemed paralyzed. Millions of people had no jobs and feared they would not be able to keep food on their tables and a roof over their heads.

A large segment of the public blamed President Herbert Hoover and his Republican administration for not acting boldly enough to ease the desperate economic conditions. The Democratic Party now had its best chance for victory since Wilson's winning a second term in 1916. It selected Governor Franklin D. Roosevelt of New York as its 1932 presidential nominee.

Roosevelt squelched Hoover's bid for reelection by chalking up a landslide victory. Shortly after his inauguration, the new president set into motion many new programs and agencies to cope with the devastating effects of the Depression. Some of his actions were controversial, but a large number of Americans approved them. When Roosevelt sought a second term in 1936, he routed his Republican rival, Governor Alfred M. Landon of Kansas, and carried every state except Vermont and Maine.

By the end of Roosevelt's second term, the German dictator Adolf Hitler was conquering large areas of Europe, and Americans feared that the war would spread to the United States. In those critical times, many people wanted their proven leader to remain at the helm. In 1940 Roosevelt announced he would run for a third term. His Republican opponent was businessman Wendell Willkie of Indiana. Roosevelt easily defeated Willkie and became the only president ever to win more than two terms in office.

After the Japanese bombed Pearl Harbor in 1941, the United States was drawn into the war against three powerful enemies—Japan, Germany, and Italy. Roosevelt played an important role in developing the policies that brought victory to the United States and its allies. Even though this wartime leader was weary and in failing health by the time of the 1944 presidential election, a grateful public elected Roosevelt to a fourth term.

Roosevelt died less than three months after he began his final term, and Vice President Harry Truman became the nation's new chief executive. In August 1945 President Truman approved the dropping of atomic bombs on two Japanese cities, an action that hastened the end of World War II. But Americans scarcely had returned to peacetime conditions before the Communist rulers of the Soviet Union attempted to increase their country's land holdings at the expense of its neighbors. The long, frightening Cold War between the Communists and the free countries of the world had begun, and President Truman helped lay the groundwork for resisting Communist aggression.

When Truman ran for a full term in the White House in 1948, he faced three major opponents. The Republicans nominated Governor Thomas E. Dewey of New York for president. Southern Democrats, angered at Truman for strongly supporting the civil rights movement to help African-Americans, ran their own presidential candidate, Strom Thurmond of South Carolina. The Progressive Party candidate was former Vice President Henry A. Wallace, who accused Truman of being too tough on the Communists.

Almost all political experts predicted that Dewey would win the election. But Truman waged a vigorous campaign that included "whistle-stop" railroad tours in which he would stand at the back of the train and deliver blistering attacks on his foes and what he labeled the "do-nothing Republican Congress." When the votes were counted, Truman was the winner in the greatest upset ever recorded in the history of presidential elections.

The Republican National Convention named as its 1952 presidential nominee General Dwight D. Eisenhower, the supreme commander of the Allied forces in Europe during World War II. The Democrats gave their presidential nomination to Governor Adlai Stevenson of Illinois. Stevenson was the

☆ ══════ ☆

Democratic President Harry Truman took his campaign to the people in 1948 and defeated the Republican candidate, Thomas Dewey.

more eloquent speaker, but Eisenhower, fondly nicknamed "Ike," was more popular with the voters. Eisenhower defeated Stevenson in a landslide, acquiring 442 electoral votes to his opponent's 89. Four years later, in 1956, the presidential contest was a rematch between these same two men, and this time Ike gained an even larger victory over Stevenson.

The United States experienced great economic growth during the Eisenhower administration. Sales of television sets and transistor radios soared; in suburbs across the entire country, new shopping malls sprang up. Many of the freeways and highways that remain in use today were started while Eisenhower was in the White House.

In 1960 the Democratic nominee for president was forty-three-year-old Senator John F. Kennedy of Massachusetts. His Republican rival was Richard M. Nixon, who had served as a California congressman, as a senator, and as Eisenhower's vice president for two terms. The fiercely contested campaign was highlighted by four televised debates between Nixon and Kennedy—the first TV debates between presidential candidates.

A record-breaking 68,828,960 Americans cast their ballots in the 1960 election, and the final tally showed Kennedy winning the popular vote by a scant 114,673 votes (49.72 percent for Kennedy, 49.55 percent for Nixon, and .73 percent for minor-party candidates). Kennedy won the electoral vote, 303 to 219, but captured eight states by less than 2 percent of the popular vote. If Nixon had won just two of these states—Illinois and Texas—he would have become president.

President Kennedy launched the Peace Corps to help people in underdeveloped countries, and the Alliance for Progress to aid our neighbors in Latin America. Courageously he forced the Soviets to back down when the 1962 Cuban Missile Crisis threatened the outbreak of a nuclear war. But in November 1963 the youthful president was assassinated, and as a stunned nation mourned, Vice President Lyndon B. Johnson assumed the highest office in the land.

President Johnson pushed through Congress the most far-reaching civil rights acts in history and inaugurated the Great Society—a huge, expensive program to help poor people, provide educational opportunities, and improve the environment. In 1964, when he ran for another term in the White House, Johnson gained a landslide victory over Republican Senator Barry Goldwater of Arizona, whom many voters believed was extremely conservative.

Beginning in 1965, President Johnson greatly escalated American participation in the Vietnam War, and his popularity with the voters sank sharply. As the 1968 presidential election approached, Republicans felt they had a good chance to regain the White House. For the second time they nominated Nixon for the presidency.

Vice President Hubert Humphrey was the Democrats' choice for president in 1968. A third politician, popular among white voters, especially in the South, entered the race. He was George Wallace, the former governor of Alabama and the candidate of his personally created American Independent Party.

Nixon won 301 electoral votes to 191 for Humphrey and 46 for Wallace, but the popular vote showed that the election was very close in some states. Nixon received 43.42 percent of the popular vote to Humphrey's 42.72 percent and Wallace's 13.53 percent.

In 1972 Nixon won a second term by trouncing Democratic Senator George McGovern of South Dakota. McGovern captured only Massachusetts and the District of Columbia.

The disclosure of the sordid Watergate scandals midway in Nixon's second term forced the president to become the first chief executive in history to resign his office. After Nixon left the White House in August 1974, Vice President Gerald R. Ford assumed the presidency.

The public was enraged by the Watergate affair. Many Americans wanted the next president to be an "outsider," someone who had no connections to Watergate's criminal activities that sent twenty-five Washington, D.C., insiders to prison. In 1976 the Democratic Party selected Jimmy Carter, the former governor of Georgia, as its presidential nominee. President Ford was his Republican rival. The election was close, but Carter won a narrow victory.

At the time that he sought reelection in 1980, President Carter was blamed for being unable to control rising inflation and unemployment. Many people also felt his leadership was flawed by his failure to obtain the release of fifty-two Americans who had been held hostage for many months after their capture at the U.S. embassy in Iran.

Against Carter the Republicans ran sixty-nine-year-old Ronald Reagan, the former governor of California. His long-time experience as a popular movie and television actor helped

Democratic President Jimmy Carter lost the 1980 election in part because he had been unable to free U.S. hostages being held in Iran since November 1979.

Reagan to charm the public. He spoke so eloquently and persuasively that he became known as the "Great Communicator." Reagan defeated Carter in the 1980 election, and in 1984 he was reelected by a huge majority. Former Vice President Walter Mondale, the Democratic nominee, carried only his home state of Minnesota and the District of Columbia. The Democratic vice presidential candidate in 1984 was Representative Geraldine Ferraro of New York, the first woman nominated by a major party for one of the nation's two highest offices.

President Reagan's administration ended some government programs, helped reduce inflation, lowered income taxes for many people, and promoted national pride and the importance of family values. Concerned about the armed power of the Soviet Union, Reagan supported the largest peacetime military buildup in American history. The combination of lower taxes and higher military spending caused the national debt to nearly triple while Reagan was in the White House.

In 1988 Vice President George Bush was the Republicans' choice for their presidential nomination. His Democratic rival was Governor Michael Dukakis of Massachusetts. Bush defeated Dukakis by a comfortable margin.

President Bush gained strong approval for his leadership in the Persian Gulf War when Kuwait was liberated after being invaded by Iraq. But Bush offended many people, mainly Republicans, by first promising not to raise taxes and later supporting a congressional act that did just that. He also was hurt by an economic decline in the latter part of his administration.

President Bush obtained his party's nomination to run for a second term in 1992. The Democrats named Governor Bill Clinton of Arkansas as their standard-bearer. Texas billionaire Ross Perot entered the presidential race as an independent candidate. He stressed the need to balance the budget, reduce the size of the national government, reform campaign finances, and protect American industries in trade relations with foreign countries.

Clinton presented himself to the people as a young leader who would steer the Democratic Party from its liberal reputation to a middle-of-the-road position. He promised to reform the welfare system and pledged that the government would provide more jobs and benefits for working-class people and some form of health insurance for all Americans who did not have it.

In the electoral-vote count, Clinton totaled 370 to Bush's 168 and none for Perot, who failed to win a single state. The popular-vote count showed 43 percent for Clinton, 37 percent for Bush, and 19 percent for Perot.

The voter turnout in 1992 was 55.24 percent of Americans eligible to cast ballots, compared to 50.1 percent in 1988. A record-breaking number of voters—104,423,000—trooped to the polls in 1992.

One important political development in recent times is that the president's political party seldom has had control of Congress. Republicans were in the White House for twenty of the twenty-six years between 1969 and 1995. Yet Democrats held a majority of seats in the House of Representatives from 1955 to 1995. During this forty-year period, Democrats also controlled the Senate, except for the first six years of President Reagan's administration.

In 1995 Republican control of the presidency and Democratic control of Congress was reversed. Democrat Clinton had been president since 1993, but the Republicans took control of both houses of Congress in 1995.

For the past four decades, the national government has often seemed deadlocked and unable to make significant progress. To a large extent, this has occurred because one political party dominated the presidency and the other major party dominated Congress. This helps explain why there usually are more presidential vetoes when both ends of Pennsylvania Avenue—the White House and the Capitol—are not controlled by the same political party.

SIX
THIRD PARTIES AND INDEPENDENT CANDIDATES

No third-party or independent candidate has ever been elected president. At some time in the future, however, such a candidate may be victorious.

The power of the two major parties has been weakening in recent years. A growing number of citizens, displeased with the way the government operates, feel cynical toward politicians in both the Democratic and Republican Parties. Public opinion surveys taken during the past few years reveal that more than 30 percent of Americans refuse to pay allegiance to either major party and instead call themselves independents. Some polls even indicate that the voters who will not label themselves Republicans or Democrats may outnumber either party's loyalists. This substantial group of independent voters is large enough to decide elections, so both political parties compete strenuously for their votes.

The first minor, or third, political party was the Anti-Masonic Party. It opposed secret societies, such as the Masons, a fraternal organization. In 1831 the Anti-Masons held the first national convention to nominate presidential and vice presidential candidates. This prompted the major parties to hold their first national conventions a short time later. Although the Anti-Masons captured less than 8 percent of the popular vote in 1832 and soon faded into history, they established the tradition of holding national party conventions that continues today.

Various single-issue minor parties followed the Anti-Masons. The Liberty Party, calling for the abolition of slavery, ran presidential candidates in 1840 and 1844. It then gave way to the less extreme Free Soil Party, which opposed the extension of slavery into the territories, but its leaders did not believe that the national government had the power to interfere with slavery in the states where it already existed. In 1848 former President Martin Van Buren sought to return to the White House as the candidate of the Free Soil Party, but he won only about 10 percent of the popular vote. The Free Soil Party merged with the new Republican Party when it was founded in 1854.

The rising wave of immigration during the 1840s and 1850s, with many immigrants coming from Catholic countries, provoked a strong anti-immigrant, anti-Catholic movement. People who were determined to place strict restrictions on new immigrants formed a single-issue political party called the American Party. Its members were nicknamed the "Know-Nothings" because they met in secret and when asked about their organization they were told to reply, "I know nothing about it."

Abraham Lincoln was so angered by the intolerance of the Know-Nothings that he said they would amend the Declaration of Independence to read, "All men are created equal except Negroes, foreigners, and Catholics." However, the Know-Nothings grew in strength, electing 10 governors, 8 senators, and 104 members of the House of Representatives. In 1856 they ran former President Millard Fillmore as their presidential nominee, and he won nearly 22 percent of the popular vote but carried only one state, Maryland, with eight electoral votes. When the nation's attention was riveted on secession and slavery later in the 1850s, the Know-Nothings ceased to exist.

One of the oldest third parties that still exists today is the Prohibition Party. Organized in 1869, it campaigns against the manufacture and sale of intoxicating liquors. Its chief accomplishment occurred in 1919 when it spearheaded the drive to adopt the Eighteenth Amendment, which made Prohibition the law of the land. This ban on the manufacture, sale, and consumption of liquor lasted fourteen years, until the Twenty-First Amendment repealed the Eighteenth Amendment in 1933.

Some third parties have been based on beliefs that call for major social, economic, and political changes. Among these parties are the Socialists, Socialist Workers, and Communists. None of these extreme far-left parties has done well at the polls because most voters believe their ideas for government control of large parts of the economy are too radical.

The Libertarian Party is a far-right political party with quite radical views. It stresses the importance of the individual in society and calls for ending most of the government's present functions and programs. In 1992 the Libertarian Party's presidential candidate received nearly 300,000 votes—more than any other third-party candidate in that election.

Another third party that appealed for major changes was the People's Party (commonly known as the Populists), which was founded in 1891. Among its demands were the free coinage of silver, severe government restrictions on the huge corporations known as trusts, and government ownership of the railroad, telephone, and telegraph companies. It also advocated an income tax, lower tariffs on imported products, and an end to the practice by which companies could obtain court orders to break up labor strikes.

Appealing chiefly to farmers, the Populists ran James B. Weaver of Iowa as their presidential candidate in 1892. He did surprisingly well in the West and the South, capturing twenty-two electoral votes and more than one million popular votes.

Sometimes the ideas of minor parties are incorporated into the platforms of a major party. When William Jennings Bryan ran for the presidency in 1896, the platform of the Democratic National Convention adopted nearly all of the Populist beliefs (except that the Democrats called for government regulation, rather than ownership, of railroad, telephone, and telegraph companies). The Populists were so pleased with the Democratic Party platform that they joined the Democrats and also nominated Bryan as their presidential candidate.

At times minor parties have split away from one of the major parties. In 1912 the Progressive Party split away from the Republican Party and proposed many reforms that were opposed by conservative Republicans. Breaking away from the Democratic Party were two minor parties that wanted to curb the growth of the civil rights movement: the States' Rights (Dixiecrat) Party in 1948 and George Wallace's American Independent Party in 1968.

In a few instances, independent candidates not sponsored by formally organized political parties have sought the presidency. These included former Minnesota Senator Eugene McCarthy in 1976, liberal Republican Congressman John Anderson in 1980, and Texas businessman Ross Perot in 1992. McCarthy received about 756,000 popular votes. Anderson won nearly 5,720,000 popular votes but no electoral votes. And even though Perot also had no electoral votes, 19,089,432 Americans cast ballots for him—a vote-count record that far exceeds that of any previous independent or third-party candidate.

Some political observers believe that Perot's candidacy took enough votes away from Republican George Bush to assure the election of Democrat Bill Clinton. It is impossible, however, to know for certain how Perot's supporters would have voted had their candidate not been in the election. Television broadcaster John Chancellor, basing his information on election-day exit polls—asking people how they voted as they leave their polling places—said that "the outcome in only one state might have changed had Perot not been a candidate. Ohio might have gone to Bush instead of Clinton. This still would have given Clinton 349 electoral votes to 189 for Bush."

There was only one presidential election in which histori-

☆ ═══════ ☆

Independent candidate Ross Perot ran in the 1992 presidential election.

ans agree that a third party definitely affected the outcome. That was in 1912, when Republican voters were torn between supporting GOP President William Howard Taft and former Republican President Theodore Roosevelt, who was running on the Progressive "Bull Moose" Party ticket. Together Roosevelt and Taft compiled more than 7.6 million votes to Democrat Woodrow Wilson's total of about 6.3 million votes. Since Wilson carried thirty-seven states by less than a 50 percent margin, if Republicans had agreed on a single candidate, that candidate would have been elected instead of Wilson.

Roosevelt did better than Taft in both the electoral vote and the popular vote. Taft carried only two states with 8 electoral votes. Roosevelt captured six states and 88 electoral votes—the largest electoral-vote total of any third-party or independent presidential candidate in history. To Taft went the unfortunate distinction of being the only major-party candidate to receive fewer votes than a third-party candidate.

SEVEN

CHANGES IN POLITICAL CAMPAIGNS

The costs of political campaigns have skyrocketed in the twentieth century. The combined campaign costs of Wilson, Taft, and Roosevelt in the 1912 election were a little less than $3 million. In 1992 the combined campaign expenses of Clinton, Bush, and Perot have been estimated at more than $550 million!

Congressional races also have become very expensive. In 1994 the winners in Senate races spent an average of $4.6 million, while the victors in House races spent an average of about $525,000.

Where does all this money come from? Beginning in 1976, the national government has helped finance the major-party candidates for the presidency (but not for Congress). A minor-party candidate can also receive government funds if that person obtains at least 5 percent of the popular vote in a presidential election.

To qualify for public financing, a candidate has to raise at least $5,000 in twenty or more states, from individuals whose contributions cannot exceed $250. In 1992, after Bush and Clinton were nominated by their political parties, their organizations each received about $55 million in public funds for their fall campaigns. Perot did not qualify for public funds because accepting them would have forced him, by law, to limit the amount of his own money he could spend in his campaign, and most of his funds came from his personal fortune.

Another source of campaign funds are political action committees (PACs). This type of committee is set up by and represents a corporation, labor union, or special-interest group that raises money and gives campaign contributions. Strict rules govern the formation of PACs and the amounts of money they may contribute. More than 4,000 PACs provide substantial sums for presidential and congressional campaigns.

Candidates also participate in many fund-raising events. It is not unusual for loyal supporters to attend $100-a-plate breakfasts and $1,000-a-plate dinners to hear candidates speak.

Other campaign funds come from direct mail appeals sent out either by the political party or the candidate. Individuals often make contributions when they visit local political party headquarters. There they may buy buttons, banners, bumper

☆ ══════ ☆

Republican presidential candidate Bob Dole
at a fund-raising dinner in 1995

stickers, and T-shirts displaying the names of the candidates for whom they plan to vote. One of the clever 1992 T-shirts showed Bill Clinton playing a saxophone.

Today the largest campaign expenditures are for television and radio advertisements and speeches. One brief, thirty-second TV ad in prime time can cost hundreds of thousands of dollars. Other major campaign expenses include placing newspaper and billboard ads, printing and mailing campaign literature, and paying the rent for party offices spread across the country. Some of the party workers are salaried, but many are unpaid volunteers.

Another large chunk of campaign money goes to the candidates' staffs. These staffs include managers, consultants, professional fund raisers, pollsters, "advance" persons who select and prepare rally sites, and armed guards to protect the office seekers.

The activities of candidates have changed radically through the years. Gone are the days when all that Abraham Lincoln did during his 1860 presidential campaign was to remain in his hometown, meet occasionally with his advisers, and write some newspaper articles expressing his views. Today's presidential candidates travel many thousands of miles at a frenzied pace. Usually they travel on privately chartered airplanes, but they also use other means of transportation.

Democratic presidential and vice presidential nominees Bill Clinton and Al Gore launched their 1992 campaign with an extensive bus tour that carried them across several states. Throngs of happy supporters waved at them as their bus traveled along highways, and large crowds cheered their remarks whenever they made bus stops. Republican nominee George Bush in 1992 traveled by train to some of his campaign destinations. Standing on the back platform of the train, he was greeted by wildly enthusiastic supporters.

Day after day for months at a time, candidates are on the road, appealing for votes. Some days the contestants may appear at a dozen or more locations and address voters from sunrise until late at night. Often they get only a few hours of sleep, and sometimes they appear on the verge of collapsing from exhaustion.

In earlier times, personal appearances at rallies and in parades were the only means of direct candidate-to-voters communication. This situation has changed dramatically in the twentieth century. Political radio addresses began in the 1920s, but their appeal was often limited because the audience could not see the speaker. Television speeches became important in the 1950s and were followed in the next decade by TV debates featuring the presidential nominees answering questions. Today, nationally televised news broadcasts draw attention to candidates in short "sound bites" or longer interviews on an almost daily basis. A single appearance on television permits a candidate to reach many millions of voters.

A new way of communicating with the voters began in the 1992 presidential campaign. Clinton, Bush, and Perot all gave high priority to television and radio call-in shows. They answered questions from ordinary citizens on programs hosted by Larry King, Arsenio Hall, Phil Donahue, and other popular media hosts who had large audiences. Also, the political significance of cable television increased markedly in 1992 when CNN, C-Span, and MTV became important players in publicizing the race for the White House.

Computers also changed the political horizon. In the past, the dissemination of political ideas was largely restricted to the media, political parties, and other organizations interested in influencing elections. Today, such electronic tools as the World Wide Web and on-line services on the Internet instantly furnish information to voters about candidates, issues, and political events.

Candidates make valuable use of these electronic databases in plotting their strategies. Computers enable pollsters to conduct frequent checks on the opinions of voters in every section of the country. If a candidate suddenly makes an unexpected visit to a certain city or town, it is often because a computer has shown that his or her appearance at that place may yield additional votes.

American political parties provide campaigns that are more intense, much longer, and more costly than political campaigns in most other countries. But there is a lot at stake for every citizen in elections—local, state, and national. As Martin Luther King Jr. said, "The most important step that a person can take is that short walk to the ballot box."

PRESIDENCY
PARTY IN CONTROL: 1789–1995

Party	Number of Years
Republican	84
Democratic	70
Democratic-Republican	32
Whig	8
Federalist	4
None★	8

★George Washington's administration

HOUSE OF REPRESENTATIVES
PARTY IN CONTROL: 1789–1995

Party	Number of Years
Democratic	106
Republican	56
Democratic-Republican	30
Federalist	8
Whig	4
None★	2

★First two years of Washington's administration

SENATE
PARTY IN CONTROL: 1789–1995
☆

Party	Number of Years
Democratic	90
Republican	72
Democratic-Republican	28
Federalist	10
Whig	4
None★	2

★First two years of Washington's administration

POLITICAL NICKNAMES
☆

Nickname	Candidate
Old Hickory	Andrew Jackson
Young Hickory	James K. Polk
Old Rough-and-Ready	Zachary Taylor
Honest Abe	Abraham Lincoln
The Little Giant	Stephen A. Douglas
Boy Orator of the Platte	William Jennings Bryan
Trust Buster	Theodore Roosevelt
Silent Cal	Calvin Coolidge
The Squire of Hyde Park	Franklin D. Roosevelt
The Kansas Coolidge	Alfred M. Landon
The Man From Plains	Jimmy Carter
The Great Communicator	Ronald Reagan

THIRD-PARTY LEADERS
(Including Independents)

ELECTORAL VOTE

Name	Party	Year	Votes
Theodore Roosevelt	Progressive	1912	88
George Wallace	American Independent	1968	46
John Bell	Constitutional Union	1860	39
Strom Thurmond	States' Rights	1948	39
James B. Weaver	Populist	1892	22

POPULAR VOTE

Ross Perot	Independent	1992	19,089,432
George Wallace	American Independent	1968	9,901,151
John Anderson	Independent	1980	5,719,722
Robert LaFollette	Progressive	1924	4,814,050
Theodore Roosevelt	Progressive	1912	4,119,207

PERCENT OF POPULAR VOTE

Theodore Roosevelt	Progressive	1912	27.39
Millard Fillmore	American (Know-Nothings)	1856	21.53
Ross Perot	Independent	1992	18.78
Robert LaFollette	Progressive	1924	16.56
George Wallace	American Independent	1968	13.53

cabinet an advisory group, including the heads of executive departments and the vice president, selected by the president to aid in making decisions.

caucus a closed meeting held by members of a legislative body who belong to the same political party. The term also describes one method of selecting delegates to a national party convention—when party members assemble in voting districts to register preferences for candidates running for the presidency. Iowa is an example of a state that uses the caucus method to select delegates.

conservatives emphasize respect for traditional institutions and values and generally believe that the best government is the least government.

delegates persons selected to attend and vote at conventions that select the party's nominees for offices. At national party conventions, the delegates select the presidential and vice presidential nominees and create the party's platform.

democracy system of government in which the supreme authority rests with the people.

dictatorship system of government in which a person or small group of persons has all the power to govern.

electoral college the group of persons, known as presidential electors, who cast the official votes to elect the president and vice president. Every state has one elector for each member it has in Congress, and the District of Columbia has three electors.

electoral vote the vote of presidential electors that determines who will be elected president and vice president, regardless of whether the victorious candidate also wins the popular (people's) vote.

exit polls public opinion surveys taken on election day as voters leave the places where they cast their ballots. From these polls, the media usually can predict who wins the election.

faction a wing, or group, within a political party or some other organization. Before political parties emerged in the United States, there were factions consisting of people who shared the same beliefs.

impeachment a formal accusation for the purpose of removing a government official from office. The House of Representatives has the sole power to impeach (bring charges), and two-thirds of the Senate must vote in favor of impeachment to remove the accused person from office.

inauguration official ceremony in which a person assumes, or takes over, a government office.

independent candidate individual who runs for office without the expressed support of any political party.

independent voters persons who do not register as members of any political party.

landslide election race in which the winning candidate receives a very large percentage of the popular vote.

liberals seek to extend the power of government to bring about changes intended to improve society and promote the well-being of its citizens.

majority the candidate or ballot measure receives at least half plus one of the total votes cast.

national party convention the meeting held by a political party every four years to nominate presidential and vice presidential candidates and to write the platform expressing the party's beliefs and goals.

nonpartisan elections all elections in which candidates do not represent political parties.

partisan elections all elections in which candidates represent political parties.

party platform a written statement that expresses the principles and purposes supported by the political party.

political action committee (PAC) a committee established by and representing a corporation, labor union, or special-interest group that raises money and gives campaign contributions.

political left liberal person or group that is left of the political center. The moderate left includes many Democrats, and the extreme left includes such political parties as the Socialists and Communists.

political party organization that seeks to control government through the winning of elections and the holding of government offices.

political right conservative person or group that is right of the political center. The moderate right includes many Republicans, and the extreme right includes such political parties as the Libertarians.

primary election party members vote to nominate candidates to run for office in the next general election. They also vote to select delegates to national party conventions.

popular vote   the vote of the people in an election. The popular vote in each state determines which electors will be able to cast votes for president. Only the electoral vote decides who will be elected president and vice president.

ratify   a formal procedure needed to approve a document such as the Constitution or a treaty.

third party   any political party other than the two major parties.

unanimous vote   the candidate or ballot measure wins all the votes in an election.

voter turnout   the extent to which citizens eligible to vote cast ballots; usually expressed in both numbers and the percentage of eligible voters who voted.

Armstrong, Richard. *The Next Hurrah: The Communications Revolution in American Politics.* New York: Morrow, 1988.

Boller, Paul F., Jr. *Presidential Campaigns.* New York: Oxford University Press, 1985.

Congressional Quarterly's Guide to U.S. Elections, 2nd ed. Washington, D.C.: Congressional Quarterly Inc., 1985.

Cramer, Richard Ben. *What It Takes: The Way to the White House.* New York: Random House, 1992.

Germond, Jack W., and Jules Witcover. *Mad as Hell: Revolt at the Ballot Box, 1992.* New York: Warner, 1993.

Goldman, Peter, et al. *Quest for the Presidency, 1992.* College Station, Texas: Texas A&M University Press, 1994.

Herrnson, Paul S. *Party Campaigning in the 1980s.* Cambridge, Mass.: Harvard University Press, 1988.

Hutson, James H. *To Make All Laws: The Congress of the United States, 1789–1989.* Washington, D.C.: Library of Congress, 1989.

Kayden, Xandra, and Eddie Mahe, Jr. *The Party Goes On: The Persistence of the Two-Party System in the United States.* New York: Basic Books, 1985.

Keith, Bruce E., et al. *The Myth of the Independent Voter.* Berkeley, Calif.: University of California Press, 1992.

Ladd, Everett C., Jr. *Where Have All the Voters Gone?* New York: Norton, 1982.

Mayhew, David R. *Divided We Govern: Party Control, Lawmaking, and Investigations.* New Haven, Conn.: Yale University Press, 1991.

Rosenstiel, Tom. *Strange Bedfellows: How Television and the Presidential Candidates Changed American Politics, 1992.* New York: Hyperion, 1993.

Rosenstone, Steven J., et al. *Third Parties in America: Citizen Response to Major Party Failure.* Princeton, N.J.: Princeton University Press, 1985.

Schlesinger, Arthur M., Jr., ed. *Running for President: The Candidates and Their Images,* 2 volumes. New York: Simon and Schuster, 1994.

Smallwood, Frank. *The Other Candidates: Third Parties in Presidential Elections*. Hanover, N.H.: University Press of New England, 1983.

Wekesser, Carol, ed. *Politics in America: Opposing Viewpoints*. San Diego: Greenhaven Press, 1992.

FURTHER READING

Archer, Jules. *Winners and Losers: How Elections Work in America.* San Diego: Harcourt Brace Jovanovich Junior Books, 1984.

Cook, Fred J. *The Rise of American Political Parties.* Danbury, Conn.: Franklin Watts, 1971.

Fradin, Dennis B. *Voting and Elections.* Danbury, Conn.: Childrens Press, 1992.

Lindop, Edmund. *Presidents by Accident.* Danbury, Conn.: Franklin Watts, 1991.

———. *All About Republicans.* Springfield, N.J.: Enslow, 1985.

———, and Joy Crane Thornton. *All About Democrats.* Springfield, N.J.: Enslow, 1985.

Priestly, E. J. *Finding Out About Elections.* North Pomfret, Vt.: Trafalgar Press, 1983.

Reische, Diana. *Electing a U.S. President.* Danbury, Conn.: Franklin Watts, 1992.

Schwartz, Alvin. *The People's Choice: The Story of Candidates, Campaigns, and Elections.* New York: Dutton, 1968.

Steins, Richard. *Our Elections.* Brookfield, Conn.: Millbrook Press, 1994.

Sullivan, George. *Campaigns and Elections.* Morristown, N.J.: Silver Burdett, 1991.

Weiss, Ann E. *Party Politics, Party Problems.* New York: Crowell, 1980.

Edmund Lindop graduated summa cum laude from the University of Southern California and earned his master's degree in history at the same university.

Political Parties is Lindop's thirty-sixth book for young readers. Within recent years he has written five books in the Presidents Who Dared series for Twenty-First Century Books, as well as *The Changing Supreme Court, Presidents Versus Congress, Assassinations That Shook America, Presidents by Accident*, and *The Bill of Rights and Landmark Cases.* He contributed twenty-five articles to *The Young Reader's Companion to American History.*

Among his other books are *The First Book of Elections, By a Single Vote: One-Vote Decisions That Changed American History, Birth of the Constitution*, and *White House Sportsmen* (with Joseph Jares).

For thirty-eight years Lindop taught history and government classes at the middle-school and high-school levels in Los Angeles, where he lives with his wife, Esther. He trained new social studies teachers at three universities.